FANTASTIC FASHION ORIGAMI

Dressing Up

PowerKiDS press

CATHERINE ARD

Published in 2020 by **The Rosen Publishing Group, Inc.**
29 East 21st Street, New York, NY 10010

Cataloging-in-Publication Data

Names: Ard, Catherine.
Title: Dressing up / Catherine Ard.
Description: New York : PowerKids Press, 2020. | Series: Fantastic fashion origami | Includes glossary and index.
Identifiers: ISBN 9781725302785 (pbk.) | ISBN 9781725302808 (library bound) | ISBN 9781725302792 (6 pack)
Subjects: LCSH: Origami--Juvenile literature. | Paper work--Juvenile literature. | Fashion--Juvenile literature. | Clothing and dress--Juvenile literature.
Classification: LCC TT872.5 A73 2019 | DDC 736.982--dc23

Copyright © Arcturus Holdings Ltd, 2020

Models and photography by Michael Wiles
Written by Catherine Ard
Designed by Picnic
Edited by Kate Overy and Joe Fullman

Manufactured in the United States of America

CPSIA Compliance Information: Batch CSPK19: For Further Information contact Rosen Publishing, New York, New York at 1-800-237-9932.

Contents

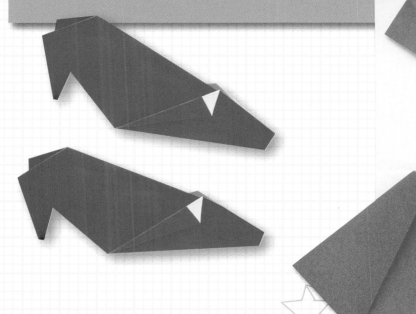

Introduction

This book shows you how to create a gorgeous collection of mini fashions. All you need for each item is a square of paper, your fingers, and some clever creasing. So, forget sewing and get folding!

Getting started

The paper used in origami is thin, but strong, so that it can be folded many times. You can use ordinary scrap paper, but make sure it's not too thick.

A lot of the clothes in this book are made with the same folds. The ones that appear most are explained on these pages. It's a good idea to master these folds before you start.

Key

When making the clothes, follow this key to find out what the lines, arrows, and symbols mean.

mountain fold   ....

direction to move paper

valley fold   -------------

direction to push or pull paper ▶

step fold (mountain fold and valley fold next to each other)

hold paper in place with finger ☞

Mountain fold

To make a mountain fold, fold the paper so that the crease is pointing up at you, like a mountain.

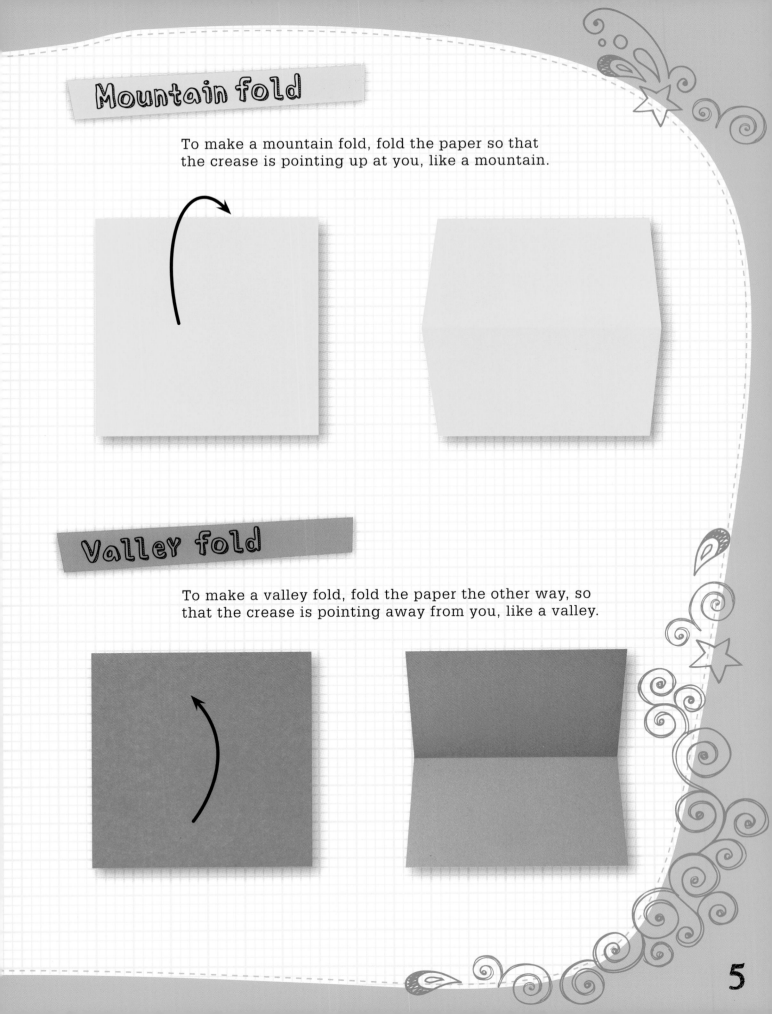

Valley fold

To make a valley fold, fold the paper the other way, so that the crease is pointing away from you, like a valley.

Step fold

The step fold creates a zigzag, or step, in the paper. It is used to divide different parts of a garment, such as the skirt and bodice of a dress.

1 First fold a piece of paper in half, from bottom to top, to make a valley fold.

2 Now unfold.

3 Next make a mountain fold above the valley fold you have just made.

4 Push the mountain fold over the valley fold and press it flat. You now have a step fold.

A step fold like the one here, with the mountain fold above the valley fold, is shown like this.

A step fold with the mountain fold below the valley fold is shown like this.

Pleat fold

Once you have mastered a step fold, making a pleat is easy. In this book, step folds are always horizontal and pleats are vertical. A pleat fold uses some creases that have been made in earlier steps.

1 To make the first side of a pleat, pinch the crease shown between your fingers. Fold it over to the right until it lines up with the crease indicated. Press it flat to make a valley fold in the paper underneath.

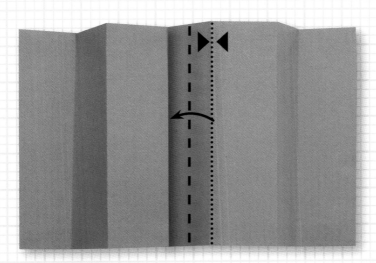

2 Repeat on the other side. Pinch the crease shown and fold it over to the left until it lines up with the crease indicated. Press it flat to make a valley fold underneath.

Hold the paper up and the finished pleat will look like this from the side.

Uniform

Fold a uniform that works for lots of jobs, such as a nurse or a flight attendant. Master the steps and you can fold uniforms for a whole workforce!

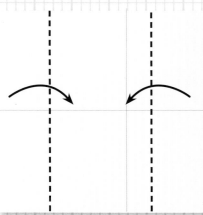

1 Fold the paper from top to bottom and unfold. Then from left to right and unfold.

2 Fold the edges in to meet the central crease.

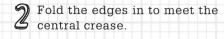

3 To make the collar, make two angled creases that meet in a V as shown.

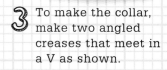

4 Shape the shoulders by mountain folding the tip of the top corners.

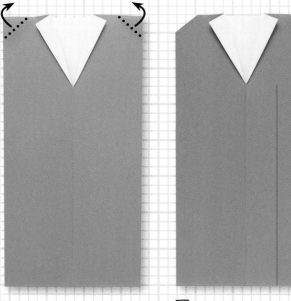

5 Turn the paper over.

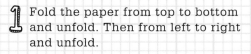

6 Make the waist with a step fold across the middle of the paper.

7 Press down on the step fold so that it lies flat.

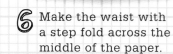

8   To shape the waist, first make an angled crease on the lower section.

9   Pinch the corner between your fingers as shown and fold it over. Press down firmly on the edge of the upper section to crease.

10   Repeat on the other side.

11

Turn the paper over to see the finished dress.

12   You now have a neat and tidy uniform ready for duty! Will it be for a nurse to wear on the wards, or a high-flying flight attendant to take to the skies?

Cheerleader

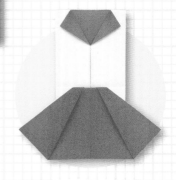

This is a fun cheerleader dress. Pick a bright paper that will really stand out on the field and prepare to make some noise!

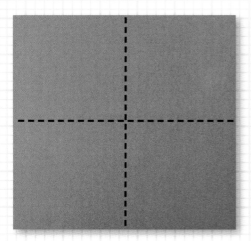

1 Fold the paper from top to bottom and unfold. Then from left to right and unfold.

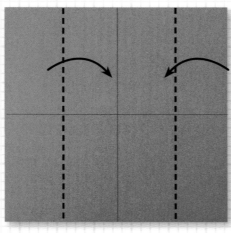

2 Fold the edges in to meet the central crease.

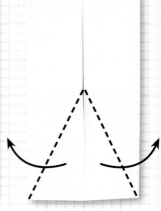

3 Make the skirt by folding over the bottom edges as shown.

4 Make the matching collar with two angled creases that meet in a V as shown. Fold down, making sure the edges are even.

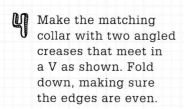

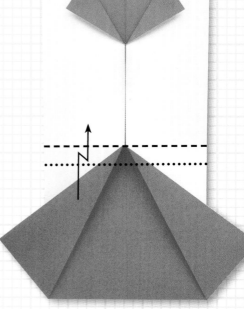

5 Create the waist with a step fold. Start with a valley fold across the central crease.

6 Press down on the step fold so that it lies flat.

7 Mountain fold ¼ inch (6 mm) from the edge on either side, keeping the sides straight.

8

Now your eye-catching cheerleader dress is ready for action! Cheer your team on to victory!

Wedding Dress

This gorgeous white gown is every bride's dream. With some careful folding you can create a beautiful bodice and a sweeping skirt!

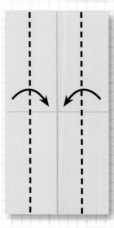

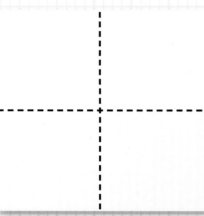

1 Fold the paper from top to bottom and unfold. Then fold from left to right and unfold.

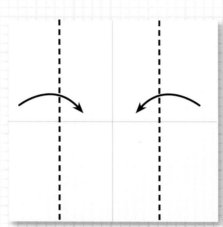

2 Fold the edges in to meet the central crease.

3 Fold the edges in to meet the central crease once more.

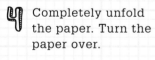

4 Completely unfold the paper. Turn the paper over.

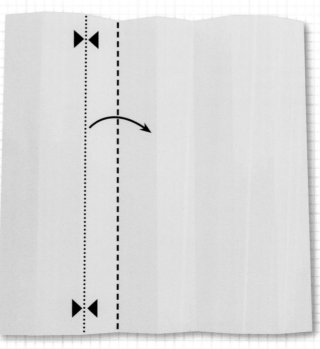

5 Now make a pleat. Take the second crease from the left to meet the central crease. Press flat.

6 Repeat on the other side, taking the second crease from the right to meet the central crease. Press flat.

7 Fold the edges in to meet the middle once more.

8 Valley fold the paper in half from top to bottom and unfold again.

9 Make two slightly angled mountain folds across the middle that meet in a V.

10 Pull the pleat to the side to reveal the paper underneath. Press down on the new creases. Repeat on the other side.

11 Make two more valley folds from the middle point to the outside corners. This gives the dress its full shape.

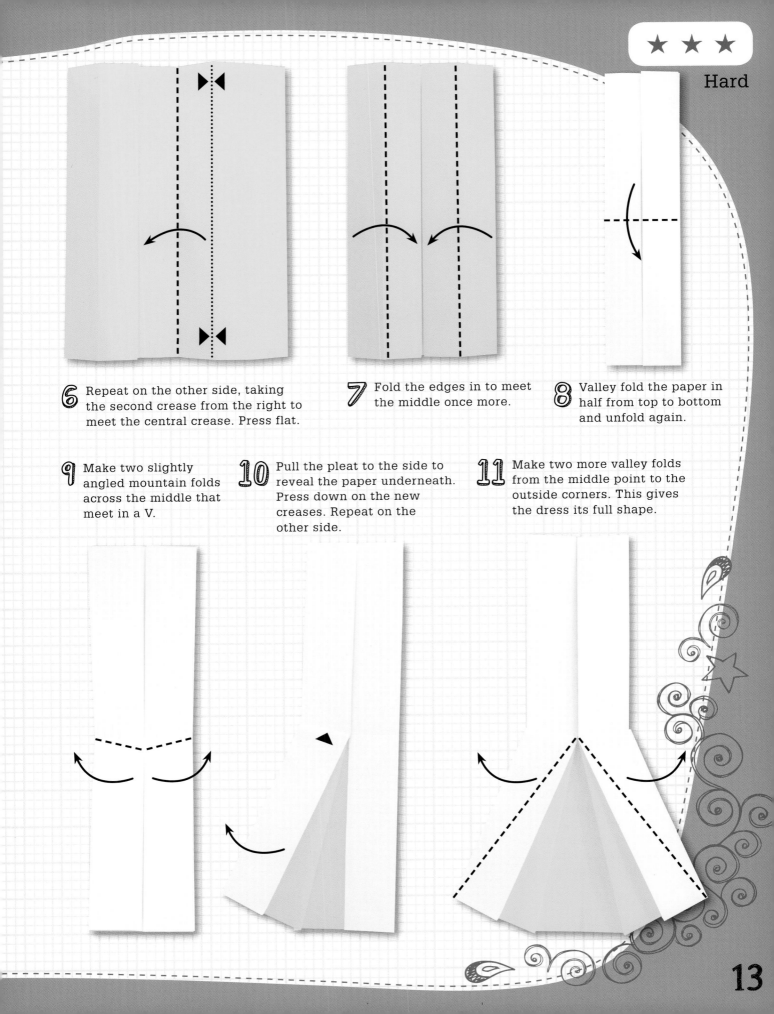

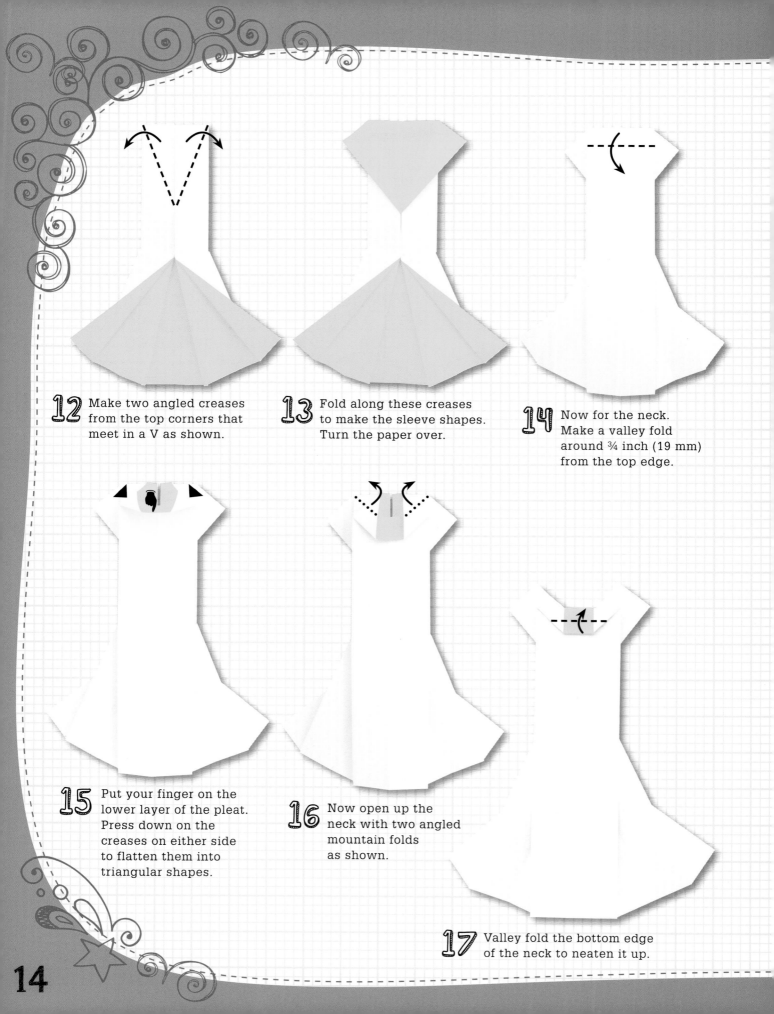

12 Make two angled creases from the top corners that meet in a V as shown.

13 Fold along these creases to make the sleeve shapes. Turn the paper over.

14 Now for the neck. Make a valley fold around ¾ inch (19 mm) from the top edge.

15 Put your finger on the lower layer of the pleat. Press down on the creases on either side to flatten them into triangular shapes.

16 Now open up the neck with two angled mountain folds as shown.

17 Valley fold the bottom edge of the neck to neaten it up.

18
Create the waist with a step fold. Start with a valley fold across the central crease.

19 Press down on the step fold so that it lies flat.

20
Make two angled valley folds that meet in a V at the central point. Press down firmly to create a waistband.

21 Now your beautiful wedding dress is ready to sweep down the aisle!

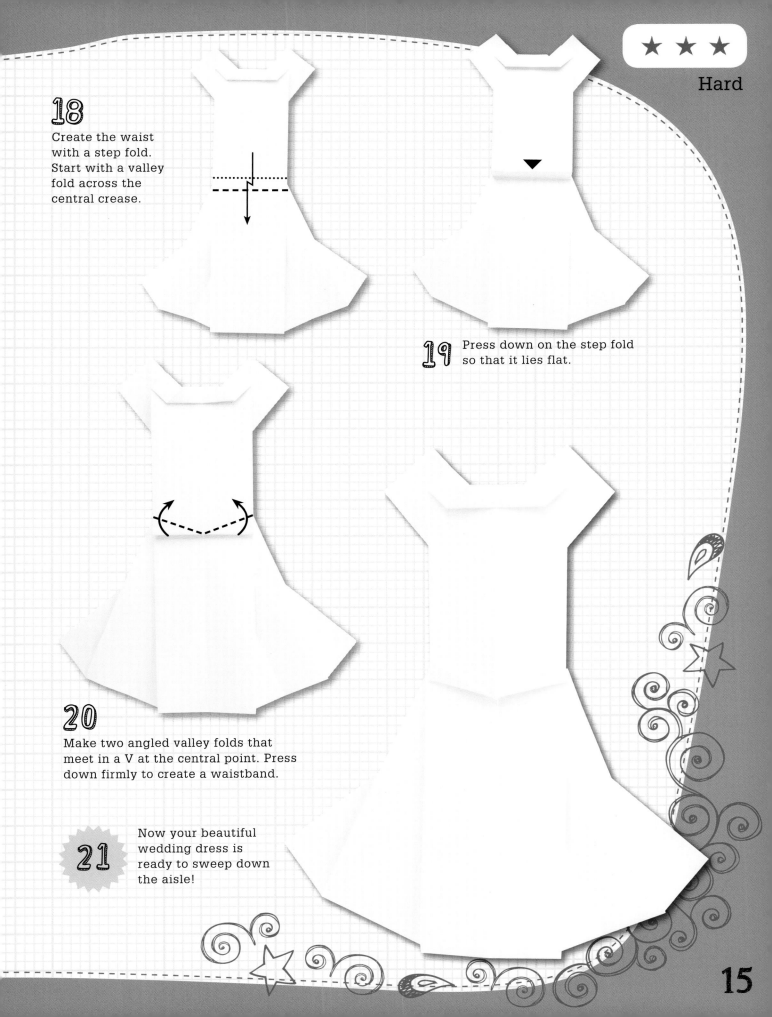

Kimono

Follow the steps to turn an ordinary square of paper into an amazing robe. Deep red is the perfect shade for this traditional Japanese garment.

1 Fold the paper in half from left to right and unfold.

2 Fold the edges in to meet the central crease.

3 Unfold the paper and turn it over.

4 Now make a pleat. Take the first crease on the left to meet the central crease. Press flat.

5 Repeat on the other side, taking the first crease on the right to meet the central crease. Press flat.

6 You should now have a pleat down the middle of the paper, like this.

7 Make a valley fold about ½ inch (13 mm) from the top edge.

8 Make a step fold as shown. When it is pressed flat, the step fold should touch the paper just below the folded top edge.

9 Make the collar by opening up the pleat at the top. Put your finger on the lower layer, then press down on the creases on either side to flatten them into triangular shapes.

10 Make a step fold in the top half of the collar.

11 Make a crease down the left side from the edge of the collar.

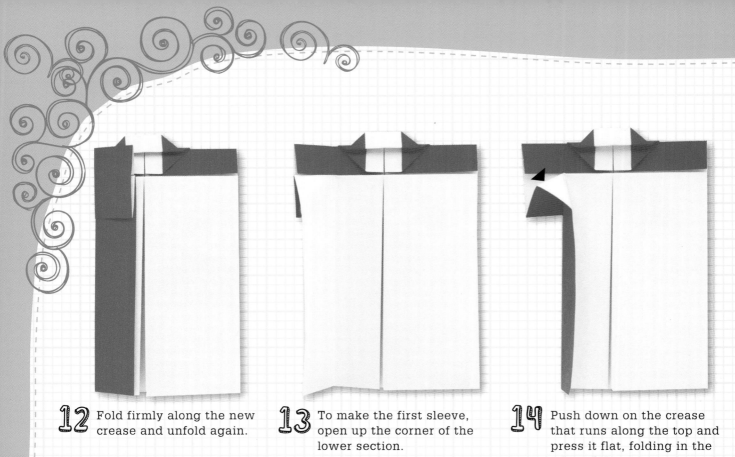

12 Fold firmly along the new crease and unfold again.

13 To make the first sleeve, open up the corner of the lower section.

14 Push down on the crease that runs along the top and press it flat, folding in the edge of the paper as you go.

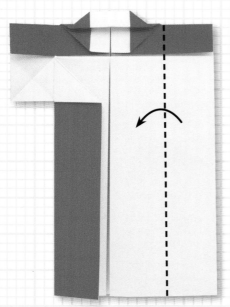

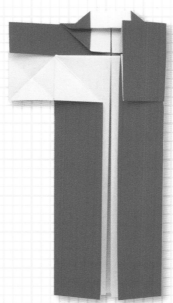

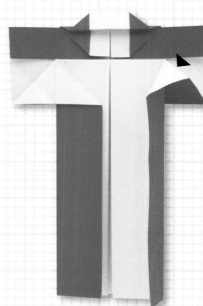

15 Now make a crease down the right side from the edge of the collar.

16 Fold firmly along the new crease, then unfold again.

17 Open up the corner, as before, and press it flat to make the other sleeve.

18 Make an angled crease below the sleeve, as shown, and fold over.

19 Crease and fold the right-hand side in the same way to make the flared robe.

20 Valley fold the tips of the sleeves.

21 Turn the paper over to see the finished garment.

22 Your Japanese kimono is now ready for a special occasion, such as a tea ceremony or a wedding.

Apron

Roll up your sleeves and prepare for some fancy folding to create this pretty apron. All you need are nimble fingers and a square of paper!

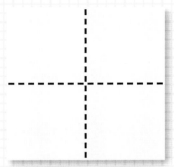

1 Fold the paper from top to bottom and unfold. Then fold from left to right and unfold.

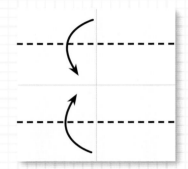

2 Fold the top and bottom edges in to meet the central crease.

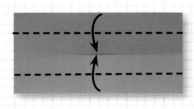

3 Fold the top and bottom edges in to meet the central crease once more.

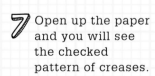

4 Open up the paper.

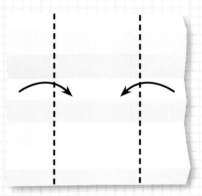

5 With the creases running across, fold the left and right edges in to meet the central crease.

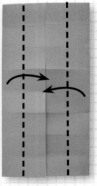

6 Repeat once more, folding the edges in to meet the central crease.

7 Open up the paper and you will see the checked pattern of creases.

8 Turn the paper over.

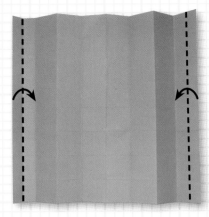

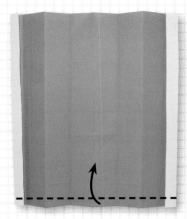

9 Fold in the left edge to meet the first crease. Repeat on the other side.

10 Now fold up the bottom edge to meet the first crease from the bottom.

11 Turn the paper over.

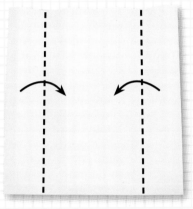

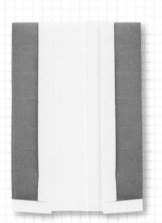

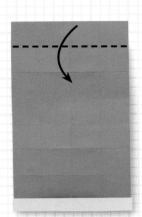

12 Fold in the sides along the second crease from each edge.

13 Turn the paper over.

14 Fold down the top edge along the first crease.

15 To make the neck, open up the top left corner and press down on the crease to flatten it into a triangular shape. Repeat on the other side.

16 Make the waist with a step fold across the middle of the dress.

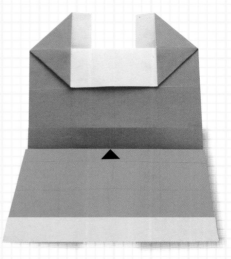

17 Press down on the step fold so that it lies flat.

18 Make two angled creases at the corners of the step fold as shown.

19 Fold and crease firmly, then unfold.

20 Turn the paper over.

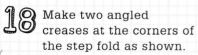

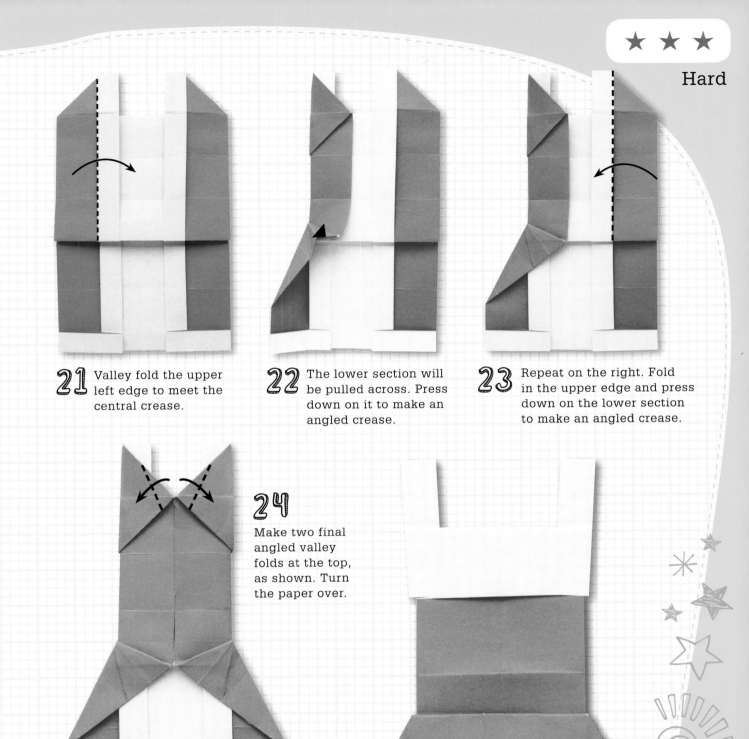

21 Valley fold the upper left edge to meet the central crease.

22 The lower section will be pulled across. Press down on it to make an angled crease.

23 Repeat on the right. Fold in the upper edge and press down on the lower section to make an angled crease.

24 Make two final angled valley folds at the top, as shown. Turn the paper over.

25 Your apron is ready for some making, baking, icing, and spicing. Don't worry about splashes and spills, you can always fold another one!

Clutch Bag

Fold a cute clutch bag with lots of style. It's handy and neat, and perfect for holding all sorts of important items.

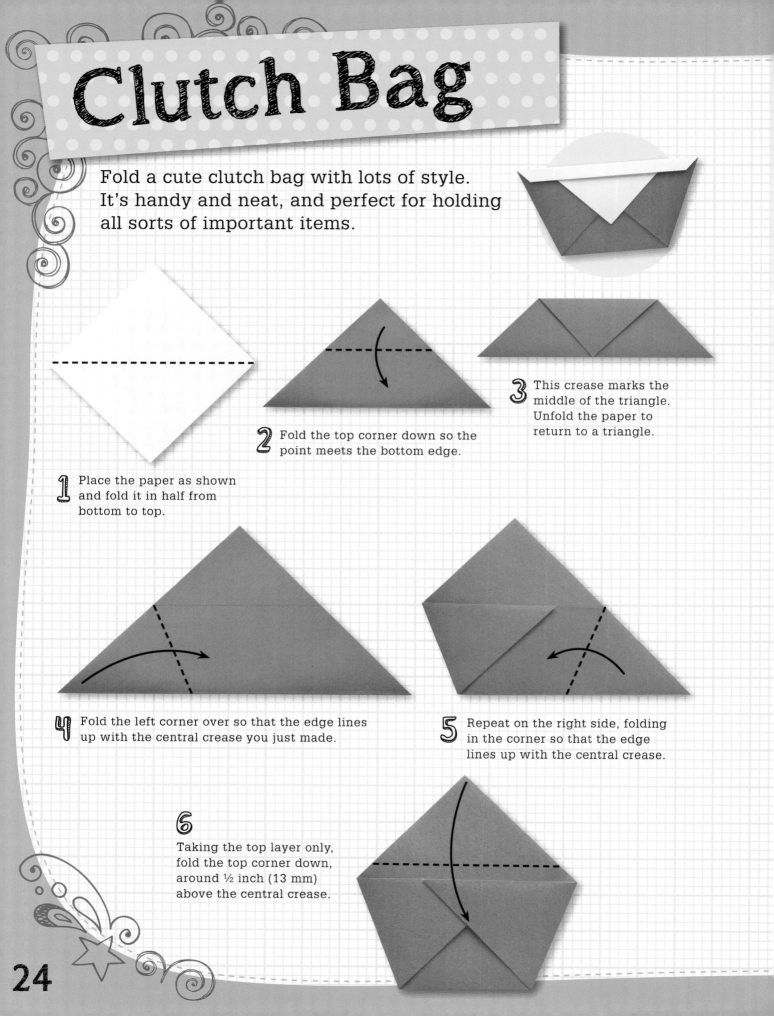

1 Place the paper as shown and fold it in half from bottom to top.

2 Fold the top corner down so the point meets the bottom edge.

3 This crease marks the middle of the triangle. Unfold the paper to return to a triangle.

4 Fold the left corner over so that the edge lines up with the central crease you just made.

5 Repeat on the right side, folding in the corner so that the edge lines up with the central crease.

6 Taking the top layer only, fold the top corner down, around ½ inch (13 mm) above the central crease.

24

7 Take the top layer again and fold it down in line with the central crease.

8 Turn the paper over.

9 Repeat step 6 on the reverse side, folding the corner down just above the central crease.

10 Repeat step 7 on this side, folding the edge down again in line with the central crease.

11 Turn the paper over.

12 Your clutch bag is complete. Open up the top and slip in some essential stuff.

High Heels

What could be more elegant than a brand new pair of high heels? Fold these right and they'll stand up on their own.

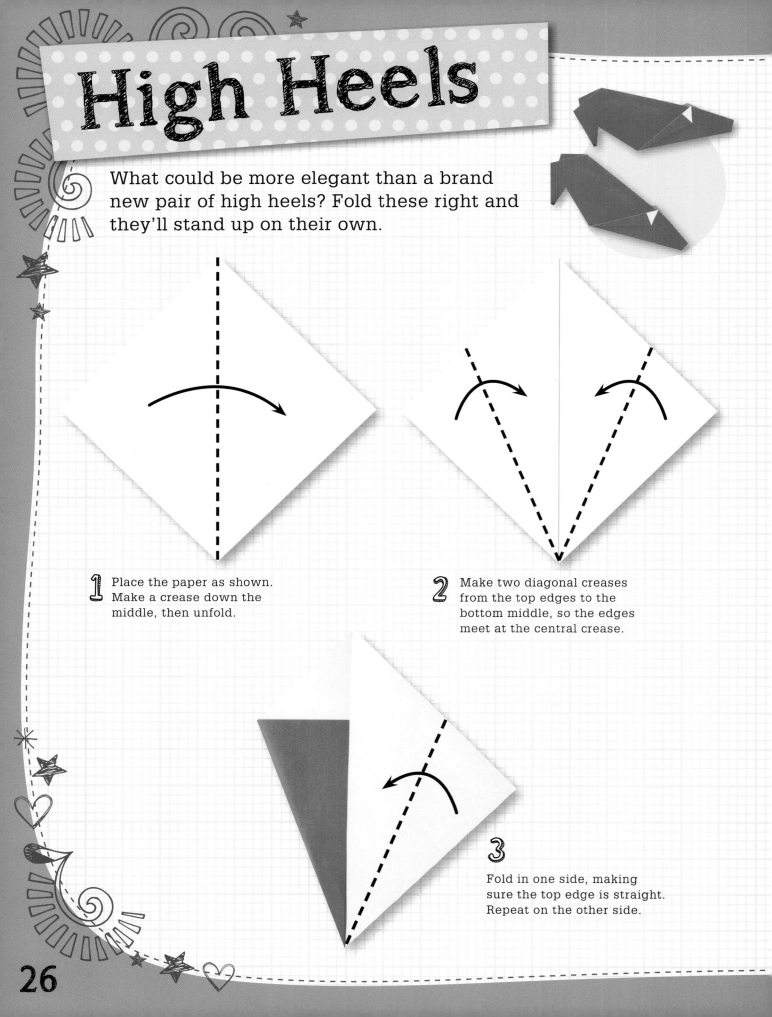

1 Place the paper as shown. Make a crease down the middle, then unfold.

2 Make two diagonal creases from the top edges to the bottom middle, so the edges meet at the central crease.

3 Fold in one side, making sure the top edge is straight. Repeat on the other side.

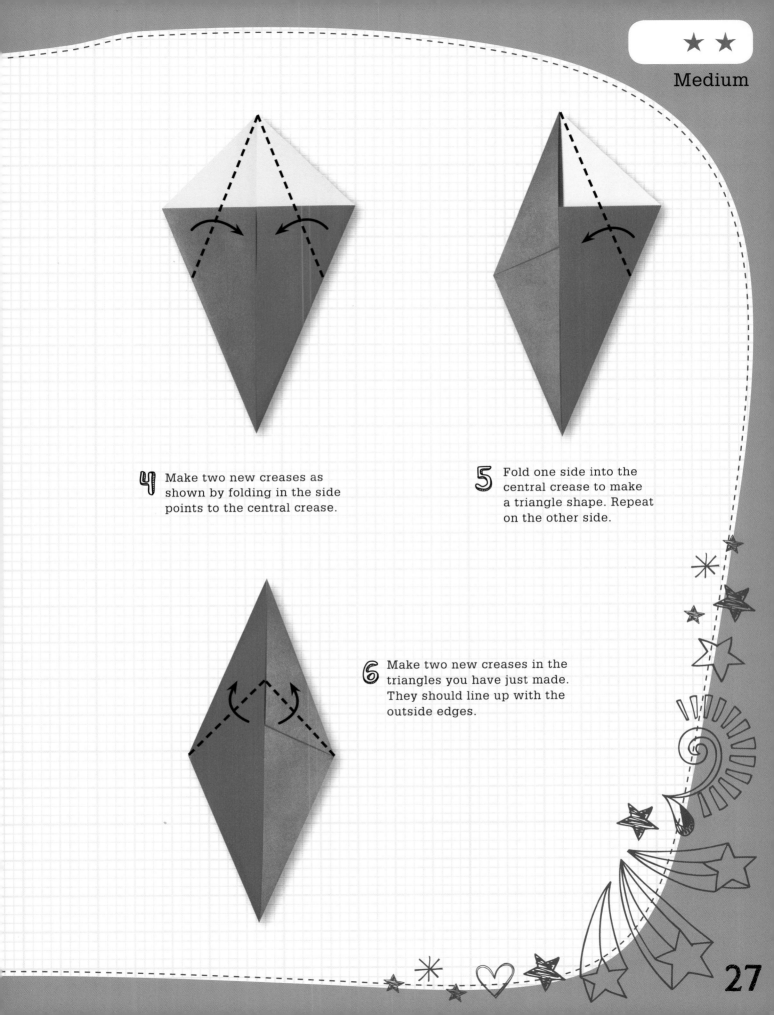

4 Make two new creases as shown by folding in the side points to the central crease.

5 Fold one side into the central crease to make a triangle shape. Repeat on the other side.

6 Make two new creases in the triangles you have just made. They should line up with the outside edges.

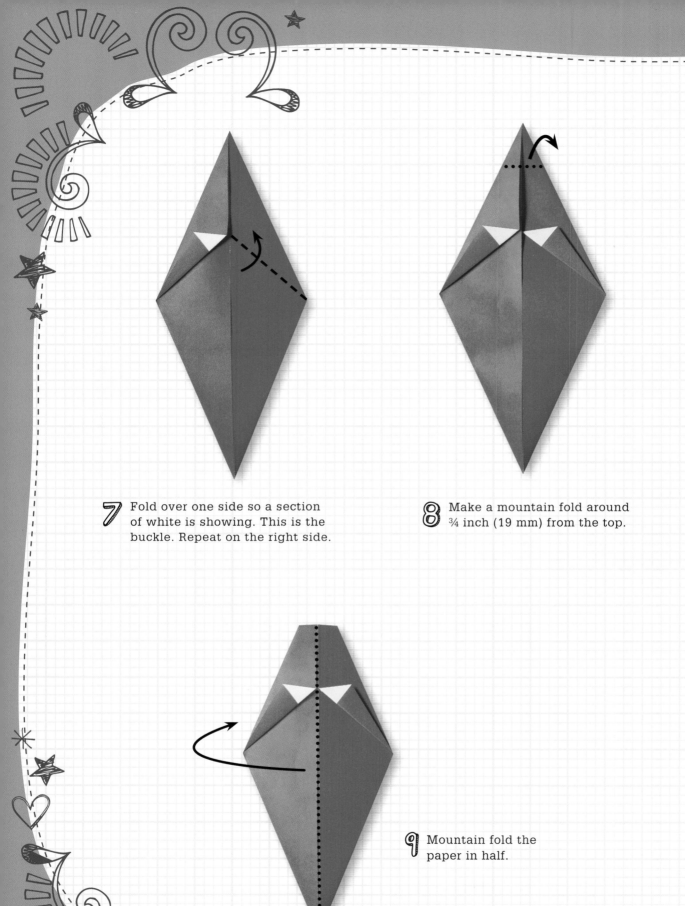

7 Fold over one side so a section of white is showing. This is the buckle. Repeat on the right side.

8 Make a mountain fold around ¾ inch (19 mm) from the top.

9 Mountain fold the paper in half.

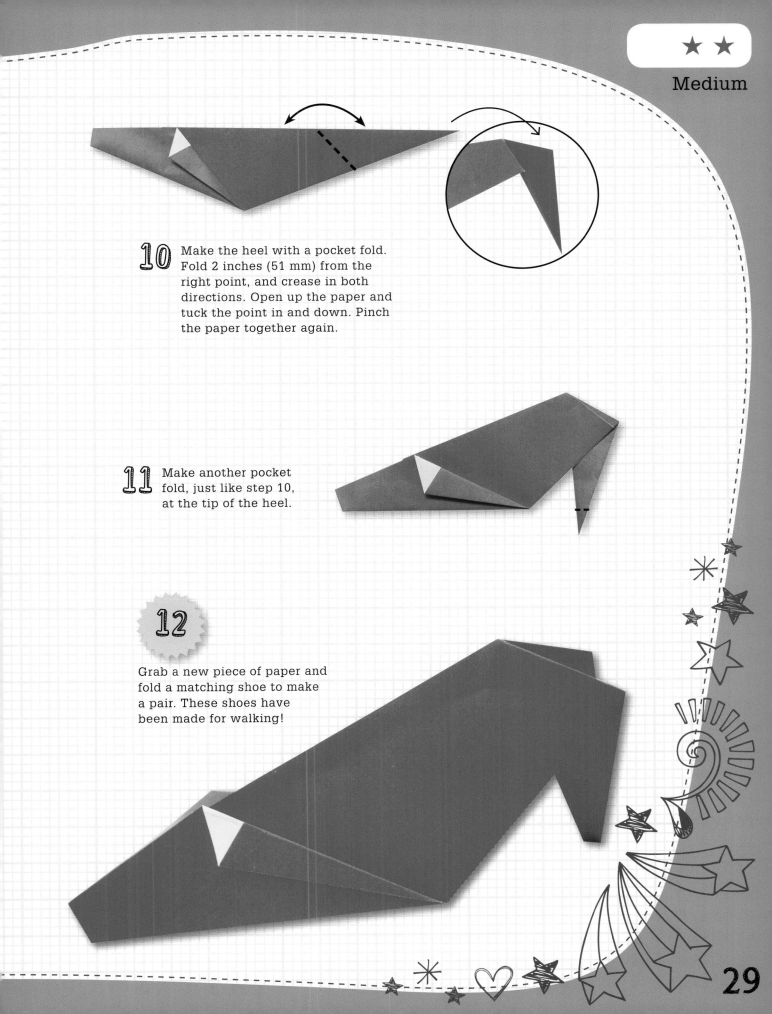

10 Make the heel with a pocket fold. Fold 2 inches (51 mm) from the right point, and crease in both directions. Open up the paper and tuck the point in and down. Pinch the paper together again.

11 Make another pocket fold, just like step 10, at the tip of the heel.

12

Grab a new piece of paper and fold a matching shoe to make a pair. These shoes have been made for walking!

Glossary

aisle A passage between rows of seats, such as in a church or theater.

bodice The top part of a dress, above the waist.

cheerleader A member of a group who performs special cheers and often organizes the cheering from crowds at sporting events.

clutch bag A small, usually strapless handbag that has to be carried, or clutched, in the hands.

crease A line or mark made by folding something, such as a piece of paper. Also, to fold something so that a crease is formed.

flight attendant A person in charge of looking after passengers and serving meals on an airplane.

garment An item of clothing.

kimono A loose robe with wide sleeves and a wide sash, worn as an outer garment in Japan.

workforce All the people who work for a company or organization.

Further Information

Books

George, Lauren Delaney. *L. Delaney's All Dolled Up: Creating a Paper Fashion Wardrobe for Paper Dolls*. Mineola, NY: Dover Publications, 2017.

Song, Sok. *Everyday Origami: A Foldable Fashion Guide*. North Mankato, MN: Capstone Press, 2016.

Song, Sok. *Origami Outfits: A Foldable Fashion Guide*. North Mankato, MN: Capstone Press, 2016.

Websites

en.origami-club.com/clothes/index.html
This website uses diagrams and animations to show you how to make all kinds of origami clothes, from T-shirts to wedding dresses.

www.origami-instructions.com/origami-tote-bag.html
Follow the instructions on this page to make an origami tote bag.

Publisher's note to educators and parents: Our editors have carefully reviewed these websites to ensure that they are suitable for students. Many websites change frequently, however, and we cannot guarantee that a site's future contents will continue to meet our high standards of quality and educational value. Be advised that students should be closely supervised whenever they access the Internet.

Index